Bitterness Because

GW01319513

Bitterness Because

Nymeria Publishing, LLC

First published in the United States of America by

Nymeria Publishing LLC, 2024

Copyright © 2024 by Rachel Finkle

All rights reserved. Except as permitted under the U.S. Copyright Act of 1976, no part of this publication may be reproduced, distributed, or transmitted in any form or by any means, or stored in a database or retrieval system, without the prior written permission of the publisher.

Nymeria Publishing

PO Box 350747

Jacksonville, Fl 32235

Visit our website at www.nymeriapublishing.com

ISBN 9798988333289

Printed in U.S.A

This collection is dedicated to all my lovers. Yes, even you.

And especially to Maria.

Table of Contents

I.

Show Me

Show me, don't tell
how your body moves with mine
how much I mean to you.
Doesn't matter if it could fill a thimble, or a stadium:
show me how much love you have for me.

You can't spin me spiderwebs in mirrors forever,
in dusty cars trace the route we will take, never go-
Take me driving along back roads, racing rivers.
      Throw rocks with me
           to the other side.
Mountain goats will follow me, a boulder trail to the bitter sea,
stop withholding these adventures
that you promised me.

Meander about how
or now
or whatever we'll do next.
What keeps you breathing,
why the sky is so blue.
My smile will stretch the clouds for both of us
and color in the shapes.

Show me what is in the bag
bind me in leather
      from shoulder
           to breast
              to toe.
Prove to me how you value my sexuality,
brush my sweaty hair away from my face
as we enjoy
the way your body
moves with mine.

So I'm waiting in the car, you say you'll be a few:
if you never want to change, my words won't change you.

Tennis Leftovers of the Day

The sky was light blue, speckled rose
like bits of salmon
I had already finished playing
In my temples the shear and strain
holding my bones together
as I eased myself onto
leaned my forehead to the fence
smelled the chalked up pennies

by clouds disintegrating
stuck in your teeth.
you were just starting.
of every piano wire
tendons twanging, muscles raw
the concrete next to the court
felt the links dig in,
and wished for a victory.

You were playing well
but sometimes that is not enough.

I took off my shoes and let my heinous state of socks wander through the
grass.
Around me people talked and laughed
but my eyes followed you like the sun.

You were
to me. You drew eyes other than mine
so my fixation was disguised.
You loved the worship, the flicker of devotion and supplication;
it is what I am.

So you were down in the set, soaked in sweat, caliginous and dark
your skin crisping up, brow rutted with frustration, potato jacket splitting.
I leapt to my feet as you approached, float, heart took too many beats
too fast, dizzying
but you are running my way, ferocity torn across your face and
kissing me through the fence, missed half my mouth
but I still grinned and breathed you in
long after you returned to the match.

I went home with my parents
but before you left, I held your shoulders
and you smiled into my neck

you went home with yours
tighter because you lost
because I won.

That was how I fell asleep in the back of a moving car
as the sky swallows the clouds, and the sun
digests the leftovers of the day.

Old Patterns

I.Climbing a Mountain

This is not the time to be sad
but the time to watch the sun rise
behind a heavy blanket of fog.
Of slowing down
of meeting at an intersection, we could have spoken but
why would we?

Beautiful things happen in the morning
when someone cares enough about you
to stumble through sleepy rays of sunlight
to kiss your forehead.
Lips press, warm
sleep smell parting
to let you in.

II.   Run

Good morning, love
time to go on a run.
Let me look at you in the *eos*, when I am ugly
and you are shining
like something the sun only dreams about.

We are at the baby rosehip week of summer
also known as
the air smells like fall and rain trembles on my forehead
doesn't sting
just falls
with no death of impact.

Do you remember those enchanting days, amongst all the others?
Days that no longer exist by thread of extended memory?
The shared narrative is gone.
Hope

where love once was
etches me away
kitten scratching, screaming
barely-there vocal cords breaking.

III.   Coffee

Love was strong.
Love was medium roast coffee, dulled with soy milk and honey.
I could never finish it all,
poured it down the girls' bathroom sink.

I taste it now and have no appetite.

Let me get you a warm drink,
let me give you that one type of chocolate that you love.
My mother's cooking, the tastes are yours to fall for.
We ensured every sense embraced, overwhelmed with creative
connotation:
candy and onigiri and gum,
learn your flavors like I learn you.

IV.   Running in Circles

This poem doesn't have an ending.
More and more people I talk to say
that they don't understand poetry.

I want to shake them.
WHO DOES? Isn't that the point?
Can't you just say that you hate looking at yourself
and that's enough?

Admit your cowardice.

You always did understand it though, maybe more than me.
Writing to you makes me remember.
The more I do it, the smoother the memories get.

The stones that have cut my soft feet
are wearing smooth
or my feet are growing calluses,
I think we know which one's true.

I wish you didn't hate me.

V.   Dreams

Come back to bed, love
Stop fighting my battles for me.
There is no end
there doesn't have to be an end.

I will sink into sleep to see you,
that's not so bad.

Blonde 2

I have blonde hair
like your favorite pornstar's
like your girlfriend's
like every girl you've ever taken to bed and, like
liked

Won't you ever look away,
don't have to look at me that way,
keep looking and
want me and
keep wanting.

Puppy stupid love written everywhere,
I used to think
I was *so* smart
with my heart
stapled to my sleeve.

If I can catch your eye I will
throw it back underhanded, you take it and

       toss
hit it
smack that shit it
sails

falls
so well, you never fell
until you saw
me.

Horsehead

Afterglow.
The room smells like stables, but instead, it's men:
chomping at the bit, members unfurled and barely contained.

Blinders on after you yank the hood off,
you are pounding down the track.
I give you   your full head,
so you can run away with   your own heartbeat.
I cling to the mane, like sweat
sliding off your back.

The panting, foaming at the mouth,
the panting, the clothes
like fallen leaves   in patterns across the floor
(like degloved sleeves)
whatever results in a winning streak.
White streaks in the bed.
Try not to think about the residue.
You lace your fingers through mine, kiss my own sweaty hair
when I kiss you.

You're my best friend.

Words:
an ice pick through my aorta.
They weigh so much more than they should.
Those hammer blows   pound molten metal,
        sink to the bottom of my dreams,
            bubble like magnesium
in bromobenzene.
Making something new   out of the same old,
same old thing.

You loved me because I was there, screaming myself hoarse.
You loved me because I dared to open my eyes
as you thundered to   the completion of your course.

Murder and Create

A time to murder
and create.

Murder
I write
because of what I create
I read
because of what I am from

When I try to put it down on paper
in simple words from my
simple brain unfurling
simply
I butcher them
slice them up with every knife in the drawer
strangling words, finding the right ones, the next one, that's it,
I want to find it again
forget where I buried the body.

And create
these words with my mind
by reading others' stories
their own murders, their own carcasses I will explore
so I can grow like fungus in the folds
like glistening beetles in their bark–
I never know when to leave things alone
when to let a metaphor die.

When to create a new story
that I will only flush down the toilet, an aborted dream,
a handmade, lovingly crafted
toilet miscarriage of a word.
God, the writers who wrote pain down after feeling it
are cringing at what I do
saying
That's really not how it's supposed to be done.

Fuck you.

I murder and create
I twist whomever's words I want
to do my bidding
and forget immediately
and do it with pleasure
and I'll do it again to fill space I can't remember.
No one is less important than I.
No one is more important than I.
I murder

I create!
I am a god! A deranged child of earth and heaven
that can see all of it,
that understands it all!

And NOTHING!!
I let the days peel back like scabs on fresh wounds
and smear the blood around
It stings.

I let the days fall softly to the floor like dandruff
dead skin
It is painless.

In burning those words, searing to brain
I only murder
or create.
In all my rage
I simply tear up,
scribble on,
or turn the next page.

Another Saturday Night

My creative bones
releasing calcium and care into my blood.
Paint me any color but red
any color than what is already there.

Leeching brittle ore from crevices lined in salt
cracked lips licking others for water.
Moisture gathers on their face

I am tired.

It has been a long day
long week.
The drugs don't work anymore
not like that.
My creative bones
creak with age
as they set a pot of water on the stove
for cooking some pasta.

The hours slow.
Solitude becomes me
It BECOMES me
It becomes ME
and suddenly
I am left alone.

Watched Pot

Don't stop looking at yourself in the mirror
watching the vines grow.
Look at the pretty flowers
Look at your cropped hair and the way it swishes the back of your neck
Listen
to what they say about it.

Skin too pale, but the sun will change that.
Something wrong with her face? Anything can change that.

Your tongue makes your teeth hurt, isn't it funny how
a muscle can move bone?
The mirror doesn't look inviting anymore, looks lonely,
looks like residue and squealing finger-dragging.

Don't stop looking for yourself in the mirror
a shirt that shows off that amazing stomach
working on those abs.
Look at how good you look and
Look at how you've grown, baby,
little baby girl, look at how you've stayed the same size
as you grow around people and are pruned at the edges.
Look at how deeply you hide in plain sight
silence and quick glances to break chains
while the links are still hot

Look at how you've
shrunk.

Stop looking for yourself in a mirror
go outside into the sun and read
go home and hide in the trees
toughen your skin with cold water and rough sand
move across the country while grasping at a silver lining
forget yourself while you still can.

A watched pot never boils
An over-scrutinized child never changes.

The Blade and the Whetstone

How do I keep my head
the blade
and not the whetstone?
Sometimes the blur lets me know for sure;
sometimes I have to guess.

I have to guess
too many times.
Too many times
for sure.

Does *this* let you know, then?

Do you hear me, with my mind collapsing at the edges?
Do you hear me, from where you are?
Tucked into a pocket,
to experience, to rip, to save
a dying deer from its prolonged death?

I am here
to hear all about it
as I degrade
whispering into the night
with what breath
I have left.

Storm Upbringing

I was born to be a storm

Slate gray skies and wind that smells of
mmm
electrons
My heart starts and stops with a lightning pulse
egg beater scream
hammered into metal and stone
so it may work as a barometer

Lose my mind to the storm

Cyclone warnings cycling through my cranium at constant speeds
build my body up to move mountains
pluck people from their perches and shuffle the deck
grinning flinty smiles, I will ruin you
Smoke you til only forest fires bellow so spectacularly
I don't mind wreaths of the stuff,
sheaves of paper and wind caught in an updraft dance

My own destruction never surprises me

but sometimes, when the dial jumps to ten and the ground won't stop
shaking
the earth won't stop quaking, crumbling, breaking
My gray eyes tarnish blue. All that is left after the storm has come and
gone
and I am the tsunami
flood of tears brimming, overflowing
wash you away, drink you into oblivion

Splitting rocks is the punishment, but it is its own reward

I will wait
in nuclear winter
to be reborn.

Part 1- California Changing

Smokey landscape
nothing taller than six inches for miles
brown scrubby bushes and ghostly transformers
buzzing with muted electricity.
My baby girl California
parched and dry!
Perception shifts as the world does,
and this green paradise will not remain as I remember it.

Young heart, lush and tall
redwood blood pumping at an ocean pace
temporal pulse.
The desert awaits farther south, so dry,
so parched that when fingers go probing
they scatter dust in flurries, or snow
that I have never truly loved.

I am wrecked, but the desert does not care.
I am alone, but the desert persists.
It stares at me, uncaring
I made it this way,
pounded my heart flat between two rocks,
(two boys)
a million boys.
Does it
matter?
The next one has his flaws,
nothing will ever measure up to the happiness I felt...
it
does not
matter.

If I can scrape away a living
among scrubgrass and empty progress
I can share my heart with anyone, but this will not mean anything to me.
Desert apathy has seeped in
and sometimes it consumes me.

I sleep and I wake up
on a blurry highway heading home.

Part 2- <u>And Suddenly, I Have No Childhood</u>

The desert
is not my home.
Home, where there is green
Home, where there is sadness and pain that I STILL have not moved
past

yet.
Isn't that the key?
Not *yet*
and in that word lies all the hope of healing, all the hope of rebirth
that love might still exist
that my future isn't etched into stone

yet.
It is still fluid, still the river
I am not the stone sinking, I am the duck playing in the water of my own
life.
The stones make the river, but the water makes the river, but really
the life that perfuses the water
slippery and wild.
The future makes the river
because it changes
and I am still changing
still learning.
There is always hope
no matter where I go.

It may dry to a trickle or disappear sometimes
I have found myself in the desert more than once
looking up, waiting for rain
looking down, wishing for flood
but always looking up once more.

College Maladies

Arthritic finger
(right pointer) indexed in multiple accounts of fuckery.
Literal: that girl is moaning louder than the TV.
Figurative: stirring the pot, licking the residue, guiding a pencil,
scratching a head.
Deterioration, a first order half life
radioactivity in the joint,
joints are harder to roll when you have never done it before
and your leading finger is swollen and stiff
for good measure.

Smoker's cough
light yellow phlegm trapped in the cave of tonsils, jolted repeatedly
trying to let it go, trying to breathe clear again.
Lungs are tired and scorched earth, burnt lead, mercury, cobalt
bronchioles so blue, those oxygen-starved anemones
waving in the wind.

Swollen ankle
Damage: unknown
Treatment: none
Cocked at a right angle and pressed into the floor,
felt something pop, something snap.
Flexion? Fine.
Extension? Agony.
Keep going, keep walking,
you have always walked off injury no matter the cost.
Tears are reserved for sadness, not pain.

Cave Boy

The city sleeps, and I am awake.
January cold works its iron fingers into shirt sleeves.
Hairs on the arm stand like feathers on a bird
and we all wish for warmth
some more than others.

The sad eyes never stop
sleepless nights of deficiency and dirty teeth.
I never saw a girl as perpetually stoned as you
cherry red, under a mask
hiding from the world.
Green cloud
hiding from us all
shrugging it all off, once again.
Vapid girl, your eyes burn like coals
scratched at and pulled raw by senseless fingers,
dull dry wood for gouging and plundering
bits and pieces.

Deeper crevices than you have ever known, cave boy
because even though your smile
is sunk so deep it doesn't touch your eyes
my heart beats somewhere
only a woman's fingers could hope to find.

Cocaine Breaths

I walk the same paths…
Pale white moon, snow never looked so white to me anyway
white as cocaine, in a little baggy
I never felt the appeal until I…

knew it'd be too dangerous for me.
Craving addiction, addicted to addiction,
addicted to the way I feel
when I feel good.
Dark grey clouds like piles of blankets swathing
the silvery coked-out sliver of a moon.

Body is tired
give me the rest.
Let the sun stream in, let it wake me up
if not warm me
Remind me what it is like to be alive,
if not more.

A numb
strong
energy.
Flattened shard of sky pressed so tightly between your thighs
the wind and the water
has become a stone
in your hand.

You sinner
Throw it.

Codfish Ventrus

I don't drink.
Not dry,
I live in wet
but I don't drink.
I don't choose it
when there are other wonderful things in the world.
When I drink, the world is less beautiful
get me out of here.

Much pain has happened.
It is a soft spot on my anemic underbelly
a blanketed white hole
in my codfish ventrus
I hate grappling the toilet for control
I hate winning, if I'm lucky

Sometimes I don't even make it that far.
Sometimes I am pissing the bed,
sometimes I am silently screaming in shame
Regurgitating my life's food in one meal that day
I am scouring my insides for matter to expel.

Small fish in the toilet bowl
Feed the fish
I cry into my arms, through my jacket

Please let him die.

Oui'd

Fall asleep
make me calm
make me eat
Still the stab of ache
push me forward so I may fall into the blanket
make me above it all, nothing touches me
when I have this secret inside.
Residing in my lungs, in my blood
in the air between us…
we laugh
and laugh and laugh and laugh

Sedate me, head so heavy I lift it from the pillow only to let it fall again.
Glazed eyes, light lulls me into dreamless nightmare.
Pool of tranquil water, viscosity 0 until green gums up the filters
and every thought
swirls into a cesspool.
Hunger doesn't exist.
I am gluttony, I am excess, I am storing food for my next winter,
next adventure called "walking around the block"
Eat until a different ache appears
until I find a combination of satiety and helplessness that kills me.

No pain, my slightly sore limbs are weightless
No pain, any position is grounding and meditative
No pain, I am suddenly flexible
No pain, I am biting at my lip,
clipping off bits of simple squamous epithelium
No pain, I am chewing my own mouth like candy,
ripping blood vessels, drinking blood

The air between us is empty
full of smoke and utterly
empty.
We laugh
and laugh and laugh and laugh…

II.

Vicks Vaporub

Can't I force it?
Tie my ribbon around his neck?
Pull it
tighter.

It looked painful.

He liked the words I haven't used before
      That's a lie. I use those words every other night; what's one more?
And every bit of love he gave me I ate,
and smeared onto my chest
like Vicks VapoRub.

He stung and I breathed in.
I'm sorry, I gasped,
while he writhed on the bed.

Sickened by his pleasure I cannot stop to think
breath torn to pant and rasp
let my fingers take over, bury my face in him.

He sweated more of the stuff and my eyes burned,
screwed up in a half-blind blink.
He reached forward, so my cheek turned
should have, anyway, I keep a strict rule of thumb:
no kiss after I stop breathing evenly,
but sometimes my lips are too numb
to notice.

They all bargain and sometimes win
This time too, because I couldn't see him
reach from behind and pull me closer
then push me on my back and bend me over-

I'll stop you there because
this is not anywhere close to a love poem.

Cigarette Boats

Now I am too aware
of the heat under these clothes
how my skin still burns because my nails are too long
Heightened in the air when the pollen first rose-
a feverish pitch of cricket song

Dirty
Neglected
I'll admit to it
of not pressing hard enough to do it
or continuing to stare past or through it
My nails tremble and shriek on the page
so after they have expressed my rage
when they scratch too hard on my neck
and leave welts the shapes of cigarette boats
I roll over in my tangle of sheets and
close my eyes

The feeling of sand between my lashes
transfers to my toes,
feel the beach underfoot again.
Because of how hot I am under these clothes
any sign of water is a welcoming end.

Blue Tissue Paper

       My chest feels blue.
The inside of my lungs are soaked and saturated,
       each rib coated;
the blood that looks crimson on the outside
       indigo on the inside.

It feels heavy, but *full*
       stuffed with wet tissue paper packed tight,
       eroding and bleeding out blue dye
seeping and staining
my stomach lining and liver.

If I tried to pull it out, it would hurt
singe my fingers with blue heat
       so I cannot move
       due to the threat of pain.

The dye is deepening into my blue blood.
I'll wake up with no moisture left
       stained with it, oily slick dye
       permeates every cell
of my sleeping body.

While I slept
       I didn't dream
While I slept
       I gathered the blue and sent it spinning out the window
While I slept
       the dye blended into the rest of the sea
and the moon
       took care of the rest for me.

Sidecar

Don't go too fast
they told me
as I sped through the boring
to get to where I wanted to go.
As if I could somehow grow through this, and into an age
where it would be more appropriate.

Appropriate? I wasn't talking about the obscene ways
my body wants to fit into yours
starting at mouth to mouth
(I've taken classes on how to save a life and that's the first step.)

I meant romantic, all the feelings balled up in there
like a bedsheet I tried to yank out
instead of slowly unwork
undoing, undoing, undone.

We can leave it on the floor
for now, but it wasn't *appropriate,* now
was it?

It was the wrong time
to wake up
to realize that I wanted to take it slow

because you had tagged along
and been dragged along
for the ride.

Fingertips

A hole in the wall.
Patched up with a shade of beige slightly lighter
than the rest of the clay-textured wall;
somehow passing that patch each day doesn't faze him.

As long as I've known him, his knuckles were scarred
bruised, oh the pain he must feel but…
is he used to it?
See the spatters on the ground, and know
his knuckles are bloody because he keeps hitting them

but he touches me with his fingertips.

There's a place on the fence that is weaker than the rest.
Looks the same as the other wood,
but the grain is smeared with skin and blood
and other humors.

When he gets mad, he hits it
hard
and the "it" is anything
has been anything
could be anything

but he touches me with his *fingertips.*

What would it take for his hand to turn?
What would it take for his mind to change?
He is fiery, it is in his nature
to flicker when the wind blows.

He hits hard
and he touches me with his fingertips…
I'm not going to just stand there while he swings.

Walls Up (In a Cabin)

I reached out
without sending nerves to my fingers
without really caring about the person that replied
so I shouldn't be surprised
when they didn't want to talk to me,
or me to talk to them.

So I choose not to feel the wall anymore
When I can, I pretend it's not there.
I try to focus that I did the right thing
by retracting my hand.

Frayed wires fade
from vibrancy,
simmering where sparks once flew.
Casting shadows on the walls, we look and reach and always tell
but never show
the affection that comes with the winter snow,
and melts so soon.
Where did our friendship go?

From warm firesides and cold hands
to icy glares and flushed, burning bodies
ashamed to be in contact, this circuit will impassion
the crevices we haven't explored, we waited
rubbed those wires' ends together to kindle a glow.

Crying Over Me

I realize that I made him cry
with my   soft, sweet-smelling hair
            small sapphire blue eyes
            thin, swollen-from-kissing-him lips
            ski slope nose and strongest jaw
That's enough to make him cry a little over me
Right?

I realize that I made him cry
with my   shyness   turning into
     teasing   turning into
        laughter   and all the
times I put myself out there
and found him bracing himself for me and
me loving him so hard
He probably shed a few tears over me

I made him cry when I said I love you
and when I broke him
It seems to him that I didn't even blink.

Statue Garden

I want to see what the world can do
if I move, unexpectedly, into the land of Greek statue?
I'd blaze up a path down center aisle
to the gates of a wedding house,
and sit with the corpses at lunch time.
When the flies circle and sweat
and everyone circles and sweats
around this lurid landscape of congealed pity and grief,
ever wondered
How could grief ever not be beautiful?

Take it to the ocean, be scarce but wipe your tears about it
No one opened their eyes while seeding full sorrow
and toss her flaky, burnt husk into the sea now
her burnt carbon. Her salvaged calcium.
Incorporating things she never *knew* into her eulogy,
make sure she's always learning.
See, the fury lashes like a clean rainstorm
dry heat and salty spatters leaking from places behind the eyes
her mind slowed
vision narrowed
and she realized she was dreaming, sleeping
standing up.

Bitterness Because

I don't have time for your hand-picked words
to convey some secret burning inside.
I get it. Your heart feels like it's on fire.
Let me cool it with my hands and push you into sleep.

You hiss like I've plunged you into water
You seem offended
It's not so deep
I don't really know what to say to that
other than

Boxes. Words are boxes. Words are limiting.

Artists
>*can grasp and tug out*
>*strands of the universe,*
>*love to twist them around,*
>*(laugh with the paint splatters and star scatters).*

So get over yourself

I live in a cardboard box.
>*I hope you live out there.*

Genuinely. I do. Because I think
you want to brave the wilderness of space and come back unaffected
Laugh at it all from a distance while you
literally wrap your arm around a star's waist and dance
to the cosmic music that plays

and you think you'll come back
just the same?

This is why I laugh. We visit, and we talk, and we dance
we will never get another
experience as special as this again
Never!

Of course, we will try again tomorrow and get the same result
and that's the beauty of living, don't you think?

Or you experience every day and are unaffected,
like it's mundane?
Never. Never speak to me again
Do not push the threads of time forward until they run together and blur
Tap each one with your finger
feel it cut like steel strings
pluck them
even if you don't know how to play, at least make some sound!

The Towel

Lately, everything that I've been writing has been about me.
So let's swing the camera away and focus on the thing behind me.
Here is

The towel.
The towel is turquoise, teal, or blue-green
The towel doesn't exactly care what color you call it
The towel has bleach spots? It is thought?
No one really knows why or how they got there
The towel is old
The towel is from Target
The towel has had many things to soak up
The towel has soaked up water, bodily fluids,
and I guess- the towel guesses- hair dye?
The towel has held blood
Period blood
but it washes out easy enough
I don't know- the towel doesn't know
how old it is
It looks old next to the others
and I
The towel
Shit you not there is another newer,
brighter towel hanging on the hook next to it
It's not just a metaphor for how the newer one is better or something
It is really hanging there.
Sometimes I
The towel wonders if it feels bad in comparison to the newer ones
I'm
The towel is
sorry
For not...
I
The towel
Doesn't know what exactly what they're sorry for
There's too many objects existing at once
There's too many old things getting lost

and not enough time to tell them that I
The towel
Love them very much
and not just the old things
the old people
The old towels
The old me
The towel.

Virginity

My celibate skin
brought before the needle.
Virgin smooth skin, they will say.
I know the layers,
secret cells in each
that house a warranted criminal
or a wronged thief
it doesn't matter.

Heartless patrol up unblemished veins
and the tattoo will burn and scrape.
No longer virgin they will say,
just as I did
when I fell in love with a voice
a face, loving hands, mouths,
so many sets of lips moving together
our bodies moving together to produce something great.

Sometimes fantasy outweighs the falls
and clouds the mind so I can't recall
the steep declines and times it was dry
but hungry fingers must search anyway.
Greedy boys ask my blank face to
do it once more
go back a few seconds, make that sound again.
My acting skills are not *that* good, no one's are.
But they pretend not to hear the cries that are few,
the gaps far between
and no longer virgin, I step up with my "virgin skin"

Yet not that either.
Let me tell you a secret
written in peeling ribbons of thinly-sliced flesh.

Though scars turn white, then back to me
my own color, my own texture, bark along the tree
I can't help thinking that my skin has been sliced before
and permanently inked in terrifying red once more.

Plan B Fails

Your secret will die
on my lips,
even though it slips
around my tongue
inside my mouth,
it will not leave
my fingertips.

As I read it on a bottle
full to the swallow,
I let it wash down my throat
and now it is inside me.

Starts at the thickening of my hips...

I feel an ache.
Sometimes mistaken
for another moon,
some other dusty thorn.

Your secret will never leave me
Your secret dies within me
My baby will never be born.

My Child

The words are so sad
when I lay them down on paper.
My child wrapped in soft blankets
I gently place upon the foldout bed.
Punch the pillow a couple times
while the early gray light trickles in.

I sing softly to my fragile seed pearl
whose eyes are not yet open to the world.
Who cries with the sunrise
the light hurts her eyes
I shield her face with my hands
but the sun only climbs.
The painful words brewing deep inside me
slowly heal over, a crust of remorse
absorbed back through my own cells.

Swaddled baby murmurs for love in an empty room
because I must also clean the house and cook the meal
go off to my own work, my adult life,
much happier than the living room with the pull-out couch
would have you believe.

Yet there are times
when I dress her up in ribbons and brush her hair
parading her around at parties
that I forget what she is.
They coo at the resemblance, when she is nothing but
gentle gummy smiles and crinkled up eyes.

I forget that anything is wrong in the world
when she softly falls asleep on my shoulder.
Nodding child, I bathe her,
wrap her in garments that are a bit too small,
she's worn them a bit too long
and back to the couch on our bit of bed
to wait for the sun.

The Silver Morning at the End of the World

This little strip of cement running down the crunchy obsidian path
feels like the quiet walk
at the end of the world

I imagine walking this in the rain and cringe
Being alone
would be so much worse in the rain

I imagine a person walking beside me
crunching the silence with their feet on the rocks
I don't think I'd like it much

I imagine a meteor, a figure standing,
fake fireworks, and laughing at nothing

Someone who calls me beautiful and is stoic
and gives me his clothes to wear as my own
a person to ruin the silence and crunch on the rocks

I imagine a lot of ugly things at the end of the world.

Ireland/Irlanda

be alone
pressed up
against the mossy back of a stone
wall
in my imaginary
foggy country
in clothes
just warm enough
to keep out the damp
with a sky lost in clouds
a sea shot within my ear

*Maybe success isn't for everyone
and maybe it's not defined the same way
so is it okay if I don't do well
but if I do good?*

III.

Swim

I wake up
and for the handful of hours between the first alarm
and ordering room service,
I have no weights on my shoulders
not one bit.

Today is my ex's birthday.
Later I will text him to tell him
happy birthday, but
I haven't remembered that yet,
don't even know what day it is.

The curtains are drawn, glowing pale grey.
Probably should get up soon
but I just stay in bed and roll over
with my messy hair, underwear with holes in it
an old, snot-stained t-shirt.

For a little bit, I am a little girl
For a vast amount of time, I have a vast amount of heart
that only thinks happy
pleasant
vacant thoughts

Trying to quantify the value of
emptiness
in a string of torment.
The
emptiness
crashes into me and I just

Swim.

Routine of Hands

The routine of hands
Gathering different sections of hair at different times,
but always the same sections, same times.

Picking up plates smeared with past meals shared with love
prepared with love, dropped and shattered but kissed the fingers
of the children you dressed, cleaned, and made with love.

And retreat to the living room
sinking among the softened leather cushions
and propping up feet that stood for hours
paying the bills, paying for...
the squashed up ottoman.

Let's listen to those calloused fingers spill out your halting songs,
flat palms rubbing scuffs off the shiny piano.
We polish this Korean piano with Korean tears.
Tear stains dry into rain,
and rain disappears at night, though you can still hear it.

The hands fold together before the night ends
loving you, loving me,
forcing the window open
letting in a breeze.

It is still the summer before the storm.
It smells
like the future is bright. Hands will shape it,
write the essays, mail the admission fees, open the acceptance letters.
I will be with you for what I can.

I will miss your hands forever once you are gone.

Online Whore

Let me listen please
to the bubbles of sex group chats typing
as they don't realize that they are dealing with dangerous
underaged prey.
It makes me smile
knowing that they are safe
knowing that ratting them out would be just as detrimental for me
If not legally
then morally
because I'd rather preserve my teenage fuck-me nightlife
than my eyes, or lips, or anything else in the world about me.

I'm just out here working my corner with what I got
      (whoring)
             with my eyes
wide and searching
legs
spread to take up room
            never would I
      touch you
   but
I'm attention-whoring like a harlot and trying to justify it to myself
by helping guys and girls get off in nameless chats that don't ask me
mine.

I liked being a whore better when I didn't write it down.
If these confessions get turned against me
Two seconds to go up in smoke
and be gone.

Prices

"Prices"

One look, and hand it over
one time in a hotel room, watch how I force my body to move for you
Digging through your wallet, unexpectedly
You didn't think it would be this good
You didn't expect to like owning people as much as you do.

"We agree on a price and you pay beforehand,
and I will be wearing a mask in everything".
I finally got my dream
move over Kubrick, Kuppola, Aster and Spielberg
I have made movies of my own
and while the audience is only one,
have you ever seen such a positive reception
When he saw me next,
clapped my hands over my head and stood over me
ovations, he applauded all over my body
and left me gasping.

"I will generally charge more for bondage/bdsm stuff,
though depending on how it goes prices may change."
Because when he hits too hard I will exact my payment
When he leaves me stinging and screaming
I will extract my own venom from his wounds and
recycle back home
When brutality has given way to apathy,
I better be paid for my brain damage
I remember plenty of times my payment was a lukewarm beer.

"I like that stuff so I don't mind."

The Trains Come Easy

He enjoys humor like anyone else,
enjoys losing himself in people that are easy to talk to.
Too shy to go up higher than the thigh
It's fun.
But then they start to talk.

Light that comes easy,
a flick of the lamp switch,
instead of creating its own years to travel on
making so many of them that
they fizzle out in the brain like dying stars.

He'd rather listen to music than to the trains at night,
Because music
At least
is contained between two gate notes,
filled with board game spaces in between.

The trains never come when you think they will.
The trains are always late.

Sometimes early.
Sometimes her hands work past the gate and down,
making the trains come early.

Pushing her away, he stands and tries to collect his head
Leans against something cold and wet
The window collected with dirty sweat
And the eyes watching as she wipes her hands and
goes to catch the next train.

We're Rocks

"You're my rock," he said.
"No, you're *my* rock," I countered.
He laughed.
I said, "Then we're both rocks."

In the desert, two stones together
content to be stones, sitting together
under blistering sun, eroded away
by unended shifting ground and weather
Yet what is this?
A drop on the face
of the one on the left?
A smatter of rain… but we were meant to be *rocks*,
pull your eyes away from that storm cloud
focus on the meditative ways our bodies grind together,
wearing each other away

No, *please* look at me, not that cloud
that winked with eyes of thunder and lightning brows

The cloud that pours out in torrents when
just about *anything* happens,
then storms and rages itself to sleep, before
twisting itself into pearly white pillows and floating off
into a lovely dream.
Set to travel the world
Set to *become* every living, breathing
nonliving, dying thing in this world.

The cloud that brings ruin by the fistful and hurls it like paint
at the dry canvas of this desert

That cloud   can leave when it likes, you are trapped here
That cloud   has expressive moisture groaning from every surface,
you are stationary
That cloud is   enveloped in the current of time,
you are stuck here.

The left rock turned its eyes to the sky
and wept drops that weren't even its own, supplemented, of course,
by the storm cloud,
wrung off its coattails.

The left rock longed to look away
to turn its eyes back to the earth…
couldn't, of course,
what wouldn't they see so it just

ached.

Pisces

I will fix the bed, he says
and we will play house.
The two of us
locked in the bliss of being
alone together
after weeks of being
alone apart.
Still trapped in the amber glue that captivates fresh lovers' hearts
and slowly, turn the lights off, perform last duties,
and pretend to share a home.

He kneels before me, he rests
his head to the spot below my chest
breathes in and out, enjoying each breath,
enjoying each new way to discover me
and I am here for the discovery
For the moments dragging on in bed through the sun
and yet instead
We are inside, alone,
together, as one.

He plays the piano for me,
evoking memories that I now realize are so ingrained
so finely etched into my being
that I will never be rid of them.
That they are like my hair, to be cut off but always grow back
slowly, painlessly, until it snags and I cry out,
wishing for days that I had shorter hair
or different things caught in it

But the nature of hair is to grow
and the nature of etchings is to smooth
to untangle.
And he unknowingly falters
stut stut
stuttering his fingers again upon the beauty of the sounds he makes.

I know what to love is
I have loved in many shapes, many forms,
many smooth skins of men who have not yet grown into full grass
men who have looked at me and
touched me and
not wanted to let me go.

I know how to love to make someone feel seen, appreciated,
valued, like a king,
       like a slave,
       like he has no lasting residue on earth
       like a wiseman, that he knows how to read the   stars
       like a   god
in human form.
I suppose I know how to love for my own gain, but
I don't do that yet.

To make someone feel the way they need to
with my body
is an art.
I don't actually know what my love is
because men expect the love they require.
He wanted fast, beautiful, perfect pitch,
swelling and wheeling among his own fantasies.
How quickly I know that I am not for him
how tightly he clings to my shiny pieces
and ignores the rest of me turning to stone.

It's not his fault, he just looks into the pond and finds a mirror
While my gold-marbled silverfish skim below the skin
flashing jewel tones his eyes will never see.

Darts in the Fog

Playing darts in fog

Here
I hand you the black ones
I take the red ones

Who goes first?
We flip a coin

Alright, I will.
What is your name
We hear the *thunk*, so it surely connects
You tell me, and I smile
A beautiful name
and step out of the way for you to aim

Tendrils of mist brush the fins on the darts
and glove my hands.
Is it sweat or condensation
that makes them slide through my fingertips?
I shake and swallow the next point.
It lodges in my liver.

That will cause pain later,
right now it is my turn to step up and throw
What makes you afraid
You never answer
the dart is still sailing through the fog
lost in the question's ambiguity.

We give it time
We don't acknowledge your refusal to respond
or the gaping hole the misfire has left
Because once the fog clears we will tally the points
someone will win, but the win means nothing
because deep in the night

The dart is still sailing through the fog.

Thistle

I'm young but I've broken a heart
not in the way that you'd expect.
Like I
stepped on it by accident
or crushed it
securely wrapped it
in a towel
and looked away
as it broke.

No,
I fucking whacked it with a hammer and regretted it immediately
Looking for the pieces was hard because I
breath
        ed
mo
        st
of
th
        em
in.

They were that small.

Now instead of moving on I feel
the pinprick of thistle thorns in my throat
My lungs, years later, still damaged inside.

"Damaged" as if they're fragile,
"Damaged" as if they're anything other than my own,
ordinary, resilient lungs.
Disappointingly damaged.

If I reveal how much they still prickle under even light touch-
though lighter touch is somehow worse,
loving hands causing shooting pain more insulting than

hard pushing yielding only dull ache-
I would turn myself inside out
and make a home inside the throbbing caves of my lungs.

In there I would set about the tedious task:
approach,
sink to the knees,
using flat palms
coaxing daggers out of the fields,
using sharp fingertips
filling in the gaps.

The parting of flesh
The parting of earth
The sinking of peace into the crevices
where pain has rooted for so long.

Singular Day

3:16 pm
On the one hand, we discuss whether there is an afterlife
and how we see our place in the universe
How when it's all done, it will start all over again
and we'll get another chance in our cosmic play
The stage is set, has been set
since the beginning, which never was
and until the end
we will be broken down by the tank treads of time
that we will never perceive as we wish we could

3:20 pm
And suddenly you point to a girl crossing the street in front of us and say
Maybe life is more genuine to live blind
without counting down the seconds until it all resets itself
simply living and enjoying each moment
without realizing the moment exists.

8:32 pm
When I hold a dying woman's hand I see the candles burning low
Wax robed flames flicker once, twice, and the soul departs into the
unknown

8:55 pm
If I cry at work I am ashamed
the faces around me observe in silent confusion
Indifference
is the path I've chosen, we have chosen to care, but ultimately not care,
because we see the souls swept up every day by the
great cosmic broom in the sky
for lack of a better word
We are there to ease the suffering
yet cause some too
with factors beyond our control

10:16 pm
A woman wanted to run away with me

back in time
into my own life
simply because she was tired
and I was young and had a smile when I saw her
and part of me still wishes I could take her with me

1:27 am
And part of me wishes that I was not here to see this
But someone must bear witness so
I hold their hands until the flashing lights arrive.

7:49 am
When I hold you close to me I try not to think of the summers
I love so much
It seems like each summer separates me so severely
from the people I've tied strings to
The price of the warm air that rushes in
is losing someone I was just falling in love with
and whether fate is real or not we both can agree on time being cold
Even when the sun won't leave and the tree is so rough under our fingers
and your lips are so soft on mine.

We settle into the grooves of each other
learn each other left from right
up from down
day and night
We memorize facts about each other to form our own opinions
and as the clock ticks down to resetting
we debate whether to disappear at midnight
or rise with the shine on mountains in the coming day.

Faith, Hope, and

The gentle, sharing way a woman loves
Illustrating each intention with a fingertip,
lightly swirling on my skin
and the single best thing I could ask for is
a kiss on the nose and her beautiful smile

With men, their actions hide behind gloves
pressing harder on the fragile glass until it cracks
slicing fingerprints along the curve of my chin
The power I feel makes my heart click and whir and whiz
but overturns once I make him more docile

We shared a bed for two nights total
enjoyed each other and the way our bodies were similar
We fit well into what we were looking for
Your hair was long and blond
Your neck tasted of metal from the thousands of necklaces
rusted into a collar,
she liked to tell me how beautiful I was in her own way

It always feels like I'm going back to bed
with these boys who don't know
me wanting them means nothing, lying
It always means something to me,
but when he spoke French into my hair
widened his eyes as we discussed everything in his mind
I found myself bored
longed for the bed of a girl
and left, quietly.

May Time

Part 1

It is May
and I am ready to have my heart broken again

Because of the way he falls into me
I am falling in love
and the way he spins me around any time we are alone,
dancing to see me dance with him,
pulls me close when I am in need of being held

Too high, he asks from the clouds
or the blue cloud just below his clavicle,
Too high?
Oh, he opens his wings for me to fall into

It has been May for many months with him
when time seems to stop and there is only us
and space
and the time when I can see him again,
and he wants to see me again
somehow

I've been in love before and oh, it was amazing
the way he looked at me and made me feel seen
how he laughed and everything stopped to hear
his gentle ways of making me feel important to him

This is new
friendship and love
cookies and cream
This was the dream spun in the books,
hot springs beneath stars and exploring the woods
in cold weather
Not belonging to anyone else but each other,
maybe we could just be happy together
How can I ever tell him this?

Because he's like me: if he knows how much I care, he will push me away
I am in love now and in denial of course
but it is May for a few weeks more
and forget-me-nots are lining the forest floor,
pathways like epithelium along its arteries
and it will be May throughout the summer if I play my cards smartly.

Part 2

June is coming and I am lost
Reeling from the harshness of his shoulders
The wringing of the cloud
writhing of his body upon the bed
I am distracting myself by saying these things out loud
nursing a wounded scattered heart with my hands
desperately loosely cupped,
holding hundreds of fluttering fragments together

Heart divided
and house chopped up laterally
Like a Shakespearean drama he pushes me away,
so I made my scorned soliloquy.
I call him while drunk,
overloaded on my confidant,
listen to the music we listened to together
and cry, angry tears this time, smear it all everywhere

The woods are empty
Wheels clicking along rough roads, nothing is smooth
for his sunshine doesn't touch me anymore
I am disillusioned with him,
as it ripped away the smoke screen I pulled around my face
when I devoted my mind to him
and heart to his gentleness
bleeding to his whims
scattering strands to the wind

I'm tired of feeling lost without him already
He was a special case of love,

and I tricked my heart into thinking I could be casual
when all I wanted to do was love him until the earth spun backwards
and the moon ripped fog and waves from my own very shores.

Summer 2021

Their fingers scrape the insides of me
Hollowing me out like a pumpkin
like a melon
and scrutinizing my face to make sure I'm making the right noises
in the right places

Only their fingers, never their mouths
because we do not bow to women in this world
Women are branches made to be bent
but not broken
because nothing is worse than a broken woman
already broken in
Like old boots worn through the toes

They drag their heels, wheeling and whirring before my eyes
Clicking machines, dehumanized to focusing in
zooming in
on me.
I was never meant to be a specimen.
I never meant to be anything but a wild girl:
skinned knees
blueberries in my mouth
tousled hair around the eyes-
They see those blueberry stained lips and say other things.

I've forgotten how lonely it is to be in love with someone
and have them despise you
it hurts so bad.
So bad, baby, I've got it so bad for you
So bad, baby, I don't know what I'll do
If you despise me too I understand, this shit
I'll break your heart in more ways than one.

So this is the summer I will get my heart broken over and over again
The summer I will realize that my body is not made for
the rough touches of desperate men
looking for an escape

The summer I will curl into a ball with a paperback and
become disillusioned with the world and
its workings
It doesn't have to be summertime for this to happen
but it always is
when loneliness strikes, so I sit in the sun and
talk awhile with the grass nearby
Try to distract myself
or fill up days with work, exercise, smoke, desperation

So this time I will choose to be happy
I will reach into the circuitry of my brain and
physically rewire myself to be content
I can live with that artificiality
It is brutal, it is pure, it is necessary for my happiness
It will get me through the day without rechecking everything I have done
It will get me through the week without clutching a glass pipe
It will get me through the summer without wasting it all being sad.

Summer 2021 (Unbittered)

I can feel the bitterness leaving my body
Somehow siphoned from my blood vessels, even minute capillaries.
Like squeezing a sponge, like wringing out a cloud
nothing but lightness
and
what's this
sweetness?
The pure, clean sweetness of honeysuckle and jasmine
banana bread and cold water
raspberry fingers and sun-warmed thumb plums?

Emphasize me.
Instead of being branded with happiness
I am being unbranded from anger
The opposite of happiness is anger
The twin of joy is brutality
The sliding scale goes from euphoria to rage
and I have been lifted clean off of the tightrope somehow.

I'm back upon my safety net
my soft shimmering sheet
Crisp cotton in the wind on the clothesline
a shield for me not to protect myself with but to create my peace
my own peace
my own clarity
That is all I wanted
and I am getting there.

Rachel and Her Strays

I straighten my dress
and walk up the steps to my parents' home,
already embarrassed for what is to come
and more embarrassed
that this song and dance will continue for many years.

Rachel brings home her strays:
boys with sweet smiles who can cook,
boys who want to stay at home and watch the children
while their partner goes to work and sparks their mind together
like a car battery
doing nothing concrete, fixing nothing tangible,
restarting hearts left and right.

Rachel takes care of her sick puppy boys,
reaches into their lives and fixes them.
With her laugh, her submission,
her way of touching their faces to make them remember their first loves,
to heal them...

But they don't heal Rachel.
They don't compete with her, they always let her win.
They don't hold her hand like him.
Fuck her in public bathrooms like him.
Leave her crying on the bed like him.

The dancing in the elevator was the closest she;d felt to life again,
the twirling, the way he held her close to him,
the way he smiled,

and he left.

He was the worst one.
He wasn't one of Rachel's strays–
she was one of his.

Can't Take You With Me

I can't take you with me.
My wings are bulging from my shoulder blades
stretching the skin like a drum,
which will rip soon and the blood will come—
but they are stirring under the surface, so close to unfurling.

Right now we walk in a silent garden
lit by sunset and ebbing clouds.
Like the ocean receding from soft pink sands,
the night always laps up too quick
washes over our ankles
reminds us of our tenuous connection.
The formality
washes away all the filler, the gender and grease and makeup
to reveal
wires
connecting us

cutting into our fingers
gently embracing bone

I don't want to be skinny anymore
I don't want to feel weak and framed in by my baby bones
I don't want to be stepped around
like everyone is scared to break me

So here I go.
My wings are coming
and when they do
I will have the liquid steel bones of a tiger
and skin as tough as the leather jackets of angels from hell
Fingers snapping fire like flint,
corners of my eyes will cut diamonds

I have been stirred and plastered with the clay that sculpted first man
hair sewn in like strong hemp or fine spiderwebs
and each feather of my wings was placed there by the winds themselves

I can't take you with me
I see where you are and I know where I will be
You will cling to my heels as I strain for altitude
and as your lips turn blue and eyes bulge from their sockets
I know that the fresh spray of stars across the sky
is not hospitable for you—
it was not for the old me either.

<u>Eliot Summer</u>

I have found my own way to the Waste Land and stood there
breathing in black and white.
Pondering my worthiness,
when lemon balm and rosemary grew upon the walk
utility lurking in every frivolous thought...

Until the smell of cannabis and roses commingled among the final steps.

The items in my arms let me do something new,
each something different from the other.
Precious parcels that let me kiss Venus,
cacti and smoking purple cylinders, smoldering guns.
All at once: behind the glass, the menagerie waited,
inside the house the neighbors whispered and
waited for me to come home,
kick off my shoes and ascend

to the end of the stairs
so I unlocked the third door to heaven, my own private haven.
Gold and ant-ridden and imperfect
for one so young as I,
that I let the street soak its way to the sky.

They walk naked through the rooms
so that the peons below can see them
and choose to smile.

Hands do not falter in what they were visiting,
listing to the side
the wheels stopped spinning
and three hours and hundreds of miles away a boy is living
with no regard to who I am
or am not supporting
as once I was his and he was mine, only support, only.

I don't know if it is time to release the red tide,
watch it sweep away the stagnance.

Gut that pulls,
the ocean is the moon and I am the tide
because suddenly I am alive and dangerous,
ultimately in danger once again.

So am I ready?

Certainly not.

The morning after streams
in grey, faulty light.
There is no sunrise I have ever seen
that I did not instantly fall in love with.

The sun watched us as we caressed ourselves
and rolled out of bed as we butterflies do, unfurling wet wings
to stiffen and deteriorate in the breeze.
When you look to the trees and see the smile waiting there,
in the palm of your hand,
swallow
death to the zygoteous future in
me.
In everyone
with that empty cave inside them that they do not want occupied.

I wept, though I have never wanted children. I wept.

He paid me twenty five dollars after he had slept, and
with no touches to my shoulders to feel the muscles that weren't there,
took a bite of banana, spread peanut butter on toast
and went away, away, permanently
AWAY.

Fiancée

My fiancée understands
That when the air gets warmer, I feel a craving for the same sex.
I soothe it sometimes, sometimes take it out of its box
and run it through my fingers
Feel the threads
feel the holes,
and the eyes.

The other eyes that are not my eyes-
they know.

They understand that most days I am not as beautiful as I could be
Usually not as beautiful as I need to be
and of course it bothers me,
I just hate wearing masks-
Not even that, I just hate wasting time
there is not enough time in the world to convince me,
a surplus, even,
that to build myself a new face is worthwhile. It's just not.
My hair is immaterial
and wiry
and to wash it is... unimportant when there's so much time I don't have.

Understand that I have a crass and dirty tongue in
my brass and dirty mouth
And that secretly, I am a man who cries, and cried, and will cry, and cry
and that my lips are uneven and there are so many woes I won't go into
Just understand that I am ugly and will one day be even worse
and that I do not care one bit.

They know how I have settled every dispute that I have caused
with two quick snips,
let it flow
free like a snake in the garden
Where it can grow
with neither of our shoes mucking it up
But we cant touch it either and see it again

no matter if we want to or not-
I never want to, I need to, and so the worm is alone with only my hands-
My shoes stay drifting in the air.
My fiancée knows their status has climbed to its peak
and will only decline
All downhill from here
but all uphill from down there-
Stay down there, there's a pavilion, and summer smells
like lilac and rhododendron.

Watch Me

Watch me watch him kiss other boys
Watch me groan and roll my hands through my hair
Watch me feel something.

Watch an invisible feeling; the heart leaping in my chest
for a secret reminder of tenderness
Watch me reevaluate his eyes behind the windows
The soul behind the eyes (the windows)
is something I have broken
and the eyes, too, I have shattered.

Watch me fall in love with stripes and air
with breathing and driving.
There is not much more to be in love with
but the memory of him kissing other people.
I fall backwards into the body across from his
and try to emulate the passion in another way.

Running in a Wet Sheet Morning

Let me go silently now
When the world is wringing itself out
like a damp sheet on a clothesline
and aborted dreams are only distant figments of a nightmared brain.

When the sun and eyes work together
to capture the air around me and paint it gold
and cold winds are replaced by humidity's baby's breath
standing graces and blue water-
seeing a goddess washed up on a beach no surprise,
only the start to my own myth:

Love is not a luxury I must burden myself with.
It does not make me light anymore, makes me sink like a stone
like a snake weaving through grass,
I can admire it from afar but don't have to get too close
shouldn't at all

The world is just a wet sheet that I can press my face into and sigh
breathe in the clean, pure sweat of the morning
When I use my aching legs,
force myself to focus on some comfortable song
the dregs of the night wicking off my clothes in long rivulets
avoiding the cars.

Acknowledgements

I would like to acknowledge the shining pillars of support in my life: my parents, neighbor-grandparents, cats, friends, and partner. Without your ears to listen, words to encourage, and food to nourish, I would not have made it this far. Thank you.

Also, I will acknowledge the transgender youths who raise their voices against oppression and carve out their places in a world that would rather burn a dandelion than eat it. Keep fighting.

Milton Keynes UK
Ingram Content Group UK Ltd.
UKHW031618231124
451036UK00004B/45